Carry Darkness, Carry Light

Carry Darkness, Carry Light

Poems by

Susan Moorhead

Cover design by Shay Culligan

ISBN: 978-1-954353-04-6

Kelsay Books
502 South 1040 East, A-119
American Fork, Utah, 84003

For Jessica, Christopher, and James even though
Fiona and Tucker say it's for them.

Acknowledgments

Poems-for-All: "Luna"

Woman Around Town: "Mr. Grimshaw," " Oranges," "The Night Taxi," "Talking," "Shift," "Salamander," "Snapshot," "On Reading an Article Where a Man Says Hunting is the Only Way He Can Enjoy Nature," "Out of the Blue," "Walk," "Lessons," "Tappan Zee," "After Solstice," "Magnolia."

The Manhattanville Review: "First Light."

River River: "The Midnight Migration," "Cicada Moon."

Earth's Daughters: "Bears."

In So Many Words: A Collection of Interviews and Poetry From Today's Poets, Madness Muse Press: "Bears," "Autarkeia."

Bayou: "Water's Edge."

Epiphanies & Late Realizations of Love, Transcendent Zero Press: "Out of the Blue," "Cicada Moon."

No Extra Words: "Perspective."

Origami Poems Project: "Things that are lost," "Things that are found," "Advice," "Thieves Spiritual," "Poem for my Black Jacket," "Green," "Red," "Yellow," "Off Hours," "Downpour," and "Pentimento" (where it was partially published as the poem,"Gaze.")

Third Wednesday: "How to Burn."

Heartwood: "Offering."

Connecticut River Review: "Coyote."

Crosswinds Poetry Journal: "Blue Willow."

Feile-Festa: "History."

The Beltane Papers: "Recipe"

Danse Macabre: "Mousewine," "Fractured," "To Complete the Spell," "Ghosts at Night."

Goblin Fruit: "Midnight Streets."

Cider Press Review: "Trespass."

Contents

THREE

FOUR

FIVE

ONE

Luna

We are moon watchers.
Tracking the moon's travels from darkness
to light, without science or consistency.

We'll note the elegance of the crescent scythe
pinned among the stars, or the gothic thrill
of a moon riding indigo clouds. We savor

the names of full moons: Hunter, Strawberry,
Harvest, Wolf. Even when we are forgetful,
as we are about so much, we'll note the cast

of light in the yard as we close the curtains,
and file out the door, walking to find the moon.
Past the neighbor who never says hello, her dog

straining at the leash. Past the man who nods
to us, carrying in packages from his car. We
follow the hint of shine through fences of trees,

over rooftops of houses like ships upon the dark sea
of lawns. At the rise of the road we find it, a perfect
round of waxed light, the pocked face mystery. We

stand gazing as the hidden stars carry the stories
of the moon, there, and ourselves, here, and all
that is in between that cannot be explained
or known or answered.

Mr. Grimshaw

My daughter catches toads on summer nights
when they fill the street in front of her house.
When rain creates rivers of glistening light
beneath the streetlamps, she gathers up armfuls
of toads and frogs, ignoring their baleful stares,
trade for this thankless task. Like the curious

black tadpole she rescued, a pet store cast-off,
he grew in our home tank, exchanging tail for
limbs, gills for lungs. Named after a secret name
our youngest son gave himself one summer at five,
refusing to answer to his given name, our toad,
Mr. Grimshaw, moved among the green fronds
in his tank, fixing us with his bulging eye contempt.

How little grace afforded to those of us
who can't remember our own transformations.
When rain sang to us, when we remembered gills
in the deluge, when we could pull letters from wisps
of clouds on a summer afternoon, writing the names
we would claim as our own if we could only
remember who we were and everything
we once knew and understood.

The Midnight Migration

At night the trees came inside the house,
orderly, as if planned,
one by one.
The three Maples, the Slippery Elm, the two
Birches known to slant together as if tender
lovers, the Gingko tree with its pungent odor,

and the shaggy limbed old fir. They would shake
off their inhabitants, a flutter of birds and squirrels,
and bend their way through the open back door,
branches flattening down from the doorway's narrow
squeeze and then springing back to knock everything
off counters, tea cups and dinner plates sent flying, a can

of peas rolling into the dog's bed as he hid beneath
the dining room table. Inside, the trees would strain
to stand, unbending and slowly rising through the plaster
ceilings, the wooden floorboards. Pushing up until
ceilings popped and cracked, until floors split and gave

way to the sturdy trunks and the determined expanse
of limbs. The fir broke through two ceilings to reach
the attic where my father, up late painting, had to step
around the needling branches to fetch the linseed oil
that lent the blue pigment of a canvas sky a certain clarity,

an elusive lightness. As for me, I took pity
on the creatures adrift in the splendor of the empty
yard, opening my bedroom window to invite them in.
Settling to sleep each night beneath a spread Maple,
with the soft murmur of birds nesting in dresser drawers,

orphaned rabbits curled at my feet, and a dray of squirrels
tucked in the pillowcase. Owls perched on my bedposts
delayed their hunt, keeping watch as the rest of us slipped
into dreams. Outside the wind blew flat over blades
of grass, like a whisper seeking a listening ear.

Shadowland

That dark shape cast across a sun warmed field
of marsh grass, seed plumes of phragmites
glowing like match struck feathers. Bold,
the dark form reaches over the glittering
surface of a lake, a dead man's float undulating
in lulling, small waves, tempting you to step off
your rock ledge and join the water. Over

and over, you take variations of the same
photograph, your shadow legs stretched
impossibly long across a swimming pool, a rise
of granite, a common lawn. You, but not you,
a touch of the old magic from childhood, your
darker self imitating your movements, a capture

of sun, moon, flame or silver, neither yet both.
Maybe we recognize our shadows as those selves
within ourselves that no effort allows us to reveal.
When Peter lost his shadow, he could not fly.
Perhaps we need these darker selves to give us
balance, lest too much light convince that we
are shine alone, burning us in a false flame.

Cicada Moon

Late summer, the air soft like a tangible
thing you could hold in the cup of your hand.
No matter what the day brought, you said,
there was always that perfect moment of rose
and blues, that golden last claim of the setting sun.

A sweet chill plumed the edges of wind stirring
through the thick darkness of trees, that old
conversation of coming and going. We were
brushstrokes on the canvas of that moment. After
you left, I listened to the whirring rise and fall

of cicadas outside the windows, the night a milky
sheet thrown across the bed. Above the speaking
trees, the sky was a saucer on which the night
balanced, and the moon was a small chip
of porcelain, above my head, above my sleep.

Sun Porch

There was a window where the screen
opened like a door, and a ledge you could
stand on if you were seven or eight,
the window frame so big it held your entire
body, arms and legs stretched to every corner.

You felt you could blaze like the sun,
or that you were a lost star finding the first
step home, that kind of shine. All that was
before you was your true story: the walk
of air, the birds calling, the sky saying

take another step. You heard your mother's
car pulling in the driveway, and nearly lost
your balance, remembering then that you
were capable of falling. You folded
your sun and stars inside yourself.

Dusk, that same window. Dark climbing
from below, the crouch of bushes blurred
beneath the ink of night. A milky veil
pinned above the tallest trees, a shimmer
of sunset. In the spill of darkness, the light

struggling to hold, and you questioned
which story was yours, the one that would
have you stay safely fastened on the ledge,
or the one that claimed the air would hold you?

After Solstice

The first winter night after December 21st
comes with a promise of longer days and
shorter nights, yet the yard is pitch black
by seven. Winter is the season for waiting,
for accepting how things come in their own
time without consideration for our impatience.

We've heard the soft rounded sounds of
hoots in the small forest behind the house,
delighted by the presence of owl, a sentry
in the trees, a magical figure in our hopelessly
storybooked minds. Tonight we mute the TV,

listen again for the volley of short screams,
urgent and piercing. We hold our phones, sift
through recordings of sounds online: fox
and fisher cat and raccoon, and determine our
first guess is right. Fox. Standing at the back

door, letting cold into the house, we look up
why do fox scream? Theories are territory disputes,
or mating calls. But what if it is just a voice
seeking its own kind? Like what I have found

with you, standing beside me, whispering
as we listen to the fox. That you notice
how dusk turns the sky peach, and when
the leaves start to turn, and how, together,
we give attention to sounds in the yard late
at night, lending us their wild language.

Trespass

A Blue Morpho, sable and teal, velvet powder
flocked on pinned, flightless wings. A monarch,
burnt umber and ebony, preserved in a permanent
hover. A memory unearthed browsing a book
of entomology. A house stay with a family my mother
knew while my parents traveled. The son and his
constant friend, both ten like me, rough boys to my
brotherless point of view, loud blurs of threat
and action. We were stuck with each other.

I trailed behind them on a summer morning,
made useful by holding extra jars. Climbing over
a fence in a stranger's yard, the boys crept the long
garden rows with the sleek grace of thieves while
I stood under clouds of insect frenzy looking
for movement behind the house windows. Bees
loped through strobes of light, landing on my arms
and shoulders. I practiced stillness. The boys plucked
captures from their nets, placed the protesting insects

into glass jars holding tissues soaked with nail polish,
I ignored their wilting flutters. When a yellow butterfly
drifted past my statue self, I caught it in an open jar.
A beauty, the boys said. At the house, we looked up
each find in well-thumbed reference books, they wrote
the common and Latin names in careful print. We
roamed the yards of strangers all week, taking turns
with nets and jars. Drank chocolate milk while watching
cartoons, avoided chores and adults. In the fall,

back at school, we acknowledged each other with brief nods, returning to our separate lives except at recess. They kept the tough boys from throwing dodge balls at my head or taunting me as I sat reading, for reasons they never explained to anyone.

The Night Taxi

It's been snowing for hours
and the only people on this street tonight
are you and some woman who was also
on the train late, and the driver of the beat-up
looking Taxi waiting patiently for a fare.

Then he's driving like a madman, and when
he skids to the address of the woman, she
scolds she's been terrified. He laughs and says,
"I'm a cowboy!" His skinny legs in his jeans
slamming down on the gas pedals as the taxi
slides around the banks of snow, just you
and him now, aiming for your home. He
opens his window to let the crisp cold air swirl
in, flecked with snow, and he tells you how
he sleeps on the couch of a buddy he stays
with, he used to drink too much, and somebody
owes him money, at least you think he said that
but your heart clenched at that last skid, so maybe not.

He's seen wolves that everyone says must have
been coyotes since we're in the suburbs. He turns
to look at you, they were wolves, and he's
seen bobcats, too. You ask him to face the road
as you tell him you believe him, and you do,
as he's handed you this slice of night that he owns
which might be the only thing he has got,
but it's enough right now, this portion, the taxi
skidding down the slick roads, his fearless cowboy
laugh, and the way the street lights are shining
on the snow like bits of broken stars.

Coyote

Loping past my headlights as I turned up the hill,
all business, his feral calling card that ability
to blend into the shrubbery with a ghostly
swift silence, a coyote on his nightly rounds.

Well timed, the husband jokes, all the people
coming home from work to let out their small dogs,
open back doors for their restless cats. I wondered
if the coyote gave any thought to the current

arguments of indigenous belonging, questioning
his place in the world or at least on that road,
or if he resented having no literary peg to hang
his furry hat on, the wolf always getting

the best stories in all the fairy tales. I recalled
the predatory grace of his gait in this first coldness
of November and I thought perhaps I should be more
concerned about the dun colored rabbits

that spot the lawns who, while often nabbing
a key mention in children's stories,
in real life do not fare so well.

The Storyteller

The girl is about nine, surveying the library's
nonfiction shelves intently. She refuses
my offer of help with a frustrated flap of her arms
sending me back to my desk. She begins
to pull out book after book until she has
a near toppling assortment. I consider how
many books will have to be reshelved
with a resigned sigh. The nanny sitting
nearby scrolling through her phone, looks up
and tilts her head towards the girl, a fond look,
a slight eye roll.

The girl looks through the books, opening some
in a layered stack, propping up others so I can
see the various photographs and illustrations
of moths and pyramids, giraffes and ancient
conifers, sea shells and a map of Australia.
She steps back, hands on her hips, and begins
to tell a story out loud, each chosen page

a part of it. As she progresses, she closes
a book and moves to the next one. I am
enthralled at my desk, pretending to be busy.
The story is magnificently complex, her voice
rich with creation as she stands like an orchestra
conductor, coaxing notes out of the glossy
pages, each book an instrument to her song.

En Plein Air

See the circle of yourself
revealed in the small round mirror
you've clipped to the top of the easel,
an exercise in looking.

Breathe, your lungs expand like wings
in the dark cave of your body. All art
starts with trepidation. Inhale, exhale,
calm yourself and lift the brush.

The exercise is this simple and this
hard, look into the mirror and paint
what you see. There's the calm sheen
of the water, the dark curve of a tree
branch against the backdrop of a blue sky.

There's the shadow of a hawk
moving left to right over the lake.
His seeking cry in every bristle of
your brush as it touches canvas.

Here you make yourself a quiet part
of everything, nothing better, nothing
worse. Here you are just part
of the landscape, that kind of benevolence.

Blue Willow

In bear-scented country, a long walk from town,
in woods where the path narrows and wanders
as if trying to lose you. Parallel to the meandering
coastline, hints of brine marry the odor of pine tar
and damp earth. A random turn ends at a stand
of tall pines amid large rocks like a closed door.

The effort of climbing around them is rewarded.
A surprise of an outcropping of once cleared land
like a hand reaching out from the forest, forgotten
by all but the abrupt sea before you. The suddenness
of open space, a shock of endless sky after the long,
dark roof of trees, the new rhythm of water meeting

rocks. To your left, a drift of old boards held fast
against surrounding brush, a wreckage of burnt
timber rotted with worm holes, sanded by wind and rain.
There's a need to stand at the edge of things, to look
out as if marking your whereabouts like a pin on a map.
Walking towards the water, you stumble over a fist

of knotted weeds, notice a bit of white tucked in
a tuft of scrub grass. A piece of old china, the design
buffed by time and elements. Faint blue lines,
a pagoda, an etch of a willow tree. The shard
curved, perhaps once the lip of a small bowl
or a tea cup. Held in the palm of your hand

you feel something tugging, almost a voice
calling. Here was once a fine view of the sea.
Here was once somebody looking.

Common Wonders

In a dark time, when I became lost, the feelings
for everyone I had loved and for everything that once
held meaning left. Light of any kind was missing
down at the bottom amid the skeleton fish and nameless
things. I stayed lost until some lift of grace willed me
back. When I returned, it was the smallest of things

that held my hand. The play of colors in a quilt, flavor
of a neighbor's offering of soup and bread. Green outside
the windows. The first thrashing thunderstorm, lightning
brash in the sky. The quilt wrapped around me. I felt
the rhythm of the hours, clockwork steady, as I stumbled

back from grief where time does not exist. People want
to find a lesson in everything, but what is the takeaway
of sorrow? I could say it was the resilience of my heart,
the will to rise that carried me, but no. It was the small
wonders revealed, moment after moment. Every bird flying,

each slowly whirling cloud, the scatters of light spilling
through tree branches, the hush in the yard as evening fell.
Noticing these small graces allowed the terrible rift in me
to mend. One evening, reading to my child, I heard tenderness
in my voice replace the rote dutiful tone that grief had
assigned me. I felt the ache of love return, common, wonderful.

TWO

Downpour

When the rain sounds like
a thousand small mouths opening
and the yard is thick with green,
we'll take to the hedges,
you and me and the small birds.
We'll shelter until the clouds empty,
and the wind whisks the sky clean.
Wait until the sun wends her way home
and she finds us here, still singing

On Reading an Article Where a Man Says
Hunting is the Only Way He Can Enjoy Nature

It takes so little to enter the green world.
It asks nothing of you, willing to hold you
without fear or division as you wander in.

Stand as a plant, rooting yourself. The earth
will do all the work. The sun will find you
under its long cast, gnats clouding over
bursts of sedum and goldenrod, bees humming
as they dance along a scatter of cornflowers.

Be still and the quiet will include you,
adding your breath to this language you
don't need to translate. Feel the air on your
skin like a new fur, soft and warm. Deer pause
and raise their heads to scan the field.

Why be what they fear? Your animal
home is this place and you are already
a part of what you think you should destroy.

Touchstone

It's a snapshot come to life, this river
with its cold rushing water, boulders
standing guard around the swimming hole.
Younger, my daughter would have a net
and a bucket as she stalked glittering minnows,
now she carries a camera for the capture.
This is one of my portals back. I see her younger
self swimming sleek as a seal, hear her
brothers' yells as they jump from the rocks.
What was lost to me returns here. What is
remembered will slip away, held only
in photographs. But each time, plunging
in the icy pool, I become something born,
a reinvention rising from clear water
into open blue. A promise there is more.

Walk

You must dip into this world. Start outside your front
door, stretch your arms towards the crown of trees
like birds tracing the course of wind and clouds before
they take wing. Start to walk, one foot after the other,
small comforts in your pocket, tissues perhaps, and a bottle

of water. Ignore the babble ringing inside your head
that the world holds nothing but hardness and hardship
and heartbreak. Start with one small thing. The scurry
of dried leaves windblown in the gutter like unfolding
ancient hands, the small stone that catches your eye

among the pebbles, pocket it, allow yourself to find
small messages everywhere. Dismiss your need
to explain or mock. Walk into the small woods
reserved for dog walkers, for clutches of teenagers
seeking a hidden place. Walk slowly, note how

the arrangement of winding paths through trees
becomes a statement about how some things take time.
Broken bars of sun effortlessly shifting and altering
their light as they meet each branch, obstacles
can transform. Walk the curved paths, breathe in

the natural change of things turning from this to that,
green to decay, rot to nourishment. Walk as many
times as you need or want, set aside whatever tethers
you to the constructs of the outer world, release it
for the silence of this new language, of learning

to carry darkness and light without fear of one
or the other. When you start to feel that relief
of claiming your portion of the common pulse
of everything, call a friend who is carrying their life
as a burden, ask them to join you on a walk.

Thieves Spiritual

I use the cell phone's microphone when
I text, slow thumbs and an impatient nature,
make it a necessity. I spoke the words
"the spinach" to my friend, and it was
texted as "thieves spiritual." Which was
so far off and yet applicable in a way
to my spiritual nature, pinching from
various religions and inspirations to
create my patchwork beliefs. I wondered
if all the voicemails I have sent with
altered words and lost original meanings
are really translations from the secret
rhythms of my speech, a phrasebook
for the language of truths I am learning.

Almosts

I glanced in the rear view mirror as I shifted
into reverse, something bid me look again before
stepping on the gas. A round cheerful face with big thick glasses
peeking over the bottom of the car's rear window. Liam,
on tiptoes, the neighbor's child come to see if my son could play.

My lecture on car safety left him unimpressed, but the almost
of the moment left me shaking. What might have been.
So often a question applied with melancholy to golden moments
missed, lovers and friends that might have stayed, chances
not taken, opportunities foolishly sidestepped, the should haves,

the could haves. But what of that car that nearly t-boned us
as our car skidded down the icy hill? The undertow on that
Carolina beach? The medical test that ended up benign. The big
problem that had an easy fix. The missing child in the department
store found giggling under a clothing rack, like Liam, not

understanding what could have been lost. So many of these
almosts could have taken us out of the beautiful ordinary
of our days and put us someplace unimaginable and awful.
What almost happened. But didn't.

Salamander

She pries back the lid of an old take-out
food container and reveals him, mottled,
dark and damp. She speaks to him calmly,
my daughter, always in tune with other
worlds. Both salamander and I are
reassured, and she says I may touch him.

Because of her I have held the pinked newness
of rescued baby squirrels, eyes not yet open.
I have cradled orphaned ducklings in my lap, fed
baby rats droppers of kitten formula and let them
nap in the pockets of a flannel shirt. A homeless
tortoise kept me company as I gardened.

I met a young rooster rescued from a cemetery
in the back of her car on his way to a farm
sanctuary, tolerated an upside down koi fish
swimming in a kiddy pool she set up in her bedroom
until her careful tending enabled him to right
himself. I have witnessed a wounded bird
limp its way to her, somehow knowing she will help.

The salamander has the damp skin
of homemade pudding. His pulse throbs
through his entire body, visible. Like one
who cannot help but show who they are
to the world. Like a girl who carries her
heart in her helping hands.

Red

Sky wide and open, light sparking
off distant water as we drive past
bleached marshlands, sun-scuffed grass,
and that funky smell of sulfur. It's a
day trip, windows down, mood wide
open, too, receiving the sun's blessing.
A stop sign, that bright smack of color,
stands where the roads merge. Some
joker has slapped on a bumper sticker
that says Being Afraid so the sign
reads STOP Being Afraid.
Sometimes God doesn't pussyfoot
around and just tells you straight.

Snapshot

Snow melting on the buried lawns, only 8:00 a.m.
and it's twenty degrees warmer than yesterday.
The black road is pooling with water the same
dull pewter as the cloud smudged sky.

Driving to work, I slow and swing round
one puddle half a street wide, and I see
the sky flipped. See the tall winter stark trees
looming in new proportions and crazy angles,

a reflection hard to resist. But I drive on,
the image plucking at me, and I make it two whole
blocks before I turn back. I stand in front of my car,
door left open, engine running, trying to snag a shot
on my cell phone camera.

A car pulls up. "You alright?" My neighbor asks.
"Just taking a photo," I say. " I'd better knock it off,
last week I got ordered off a snow bank by two cops.
Got a great photo though." She laughs and drives on.

When I was a kid, I would turn upside down on the couch
to see my world in a new way. The blood rushing to my
head as the floor became ceiling and the ceiling floor.
I imagined how we'd live in our house with rugs above us,
and windows at knee height so we'd have to crouch down

for a view. To know the same place, but different. To see it new.
Like a puddle holding enormous trees climbing up a slurry
sky. A mirror made out of melted snow.
Worth being late to work.

The Explorer

Children squealed in the cold of the swimming hole,
the river never warming in its rush to be elsewhere.
Wading cautiously, my feet feeling for passage
over sharp rocks, I noticed an opening in the brush
on the opposite bank where vines arched and twisted,
forming a natural tunnel. My mind played with
what might be at its end: animals, of course,

or for whimsy, a hobbit's door, or even something
not meant to be disturbed, some absence of light
as gnarled branches denied even a sliver of this
bluest of skies. I thought to get my camera, making
my way back to our sprawl of beach chairs and towels.
Raising the lens, I saw my son poised at the edge
of the green mouth. A ridiculous fear gripped me

as he plunged into the unknowing of it. I fought
the urge to call to him, not wanting to burden
my child with my own fearful nature. I watched
other people's children jump off the great rock
thinking how my husband taught each of our children
to make that leap I never could. How my best parenting
is keeping my children from the worst of myself.

My son emerged, crossing the river, a pleased
smile on his face. Flopping down on a sun warmed
towel, he motioned across the water. He had
discovered a tunnel in the bushes and walked
the length of it. "A bit tricky over some rocky
parts, but guess what I found at the end?"
He grinned. "A secret waterfall, taller than me!"

Water's Edge

Playing mermaid and Marco Polo in the shallows, frisking
the edges of the water with sand-flecked friends; day spent
chasing silver fish so swift, only their shadows catch
in the net. Plucking hermit crabs, tight as fists
in their small shells, letting them fall with a hollow
thunk to the bottom of an orange bucket. Someone's mother
yells dinner and you look up. See him, top of the stairs,
scanning the beach, hand blocking out the sun, his jacket
the same smudge of blue as the sky.

Mother with her magazine on her lap doesn't move
when he says let's swim. She never swims. Your
sister has swum far out already. There is only you
on the beach, swallowing fear behind his shadow cast
on your face. Beside him on the long walkway, cement
buffeted by sea grass. You've heard eels lie in coils
at the roots. Avoid rough chinks where the sea
has stormed over, seeking claim. The water breaks
sleek and thick. At the end he dives, waits without patience.

You lose your life in the short dive, swallowed
by the sea, breath stolen by cold water. He turns
and begins the long strokes in. He'll stop if you cry out
but not the first time, only when you give up halfway
in as you always do. He'll let you ride his broad back
to the shore. You swim. Past the wooden float where others
sprawl and laugh, where your sister suns, her skin oiled
bronze. He is only a line slicing through the water.

Muscles twang fire as you make your arms match him,
stroke for stroke, the sea enters your gasping mouth,
thin legs kicking at endless water. Past where you first gave
up, past where you remember, only the stroke, fire
in your arms, and shadows mouthing underneath water;
constant threat hanging like a sword in the press of sky.

The surprise of being able to touch, to stand. You forgot
that was the aim, to get back to shore. He is grinning,
he is saying something, but you are looking back
at the sea, looking at how far a distance you have come.
His words fall like sand littered beneath your feet.

Four Rooms

You can climb over the walls crumbling
like chocolate cake, loamy, dirt eager for seeds.
They sprout whiskers, feel their way down, twine
around a pebble, a discarded slice of broken glass,
luring the curious worm, desire for the fertile bed
of castings. Yes, the air is fresh in this room, new,
like a first thing, yes, the rain feels cleaner, but
it's all showing off, birthing, blooming,
big deal, you've done that.

Clouds plump up as the ceiling pulls into a lean
stretch of perfect blues, cornflower, turquoise, faded
denim, blues to sink into like a hammock, drowse,
wake twenty years younger, drinking iced tea from a
mason jar, skin warming amber. Breezes tease, talk
of things untied, the taste of olives bitter and salty,
tongue curling to suck out the pimentos. You can be
so careless and it doesn't count, it's just the heat
and the way it gets at night, the dip and rise of cicada
song, scratching rhythms of katydids, crickets,
all those noisy bugs itchy with insomnia.

A turn of heart, you wander north. A house
hidden deep in complicated woods, mottled
yellow walls and a verdigris roof. Inside,
dark interiors cool your fevered skin, stories
paper the walls as memories fly in and out
of the windows like birds whose names
you have forgotten. Footsteps on the stairs,
someone is leaving. A calico cat stares
at something you can't see.

An iron door, a dangling chain. You push
and it shudders open, rusted hinges complaining
after years of neglect. A dark sky, the blankness
of cold, snow falling without rhythm or music.
All the questions you thought needed answers
are silent. You've been here before.

Rainswept

Windows blurred, no visibility. We sit in the egg
of the car and try to creep down this mountain
road to some side place we can hole up. The sky

is a hurl of water, hot with lightning, a thundering
giant stomping out of myths. Wind pummels
the car, tosses branches, slaps of leaves, scraping

the roof as the car shudders, skidding wheels spin
in the sudden mud. The rear view mirror holds
the faces of our children staring at the crazed sky,

rocked in this cradle of static and crash. We shout lies
of assurance, they huddle in the back seat, notice
their father's grip on the steering wheel, their mother's wince

at each blinding flash. They count, we hear them count,
until the seconds between crash and light stretch out in their
combined voices, and the wipers lessen their frantic pace

on the windshield. We breathe, we look at each other,
shaken and wordless, as blue steals into the wind-whisked
sky and clouds trudge away their suitcase of rain.

First Light

I know this sound, first birds of morning.
As a child, I waited hours for the drape
of night to roll up again. Leaning into the first
hint of the fresh day, the fragile lace of hesitant
light, the receding darkness dappled with bird song,
able at last to close my eyes.

I know this sound, some kind of redemption,
waking me from scattered sleep, a healing fragment
even as the work of the previous day marks my bones
in notches. Night leaves its small fur as the dawn
pushes, as the birds persist, and morning unfurls
like a promise you hoped someone would keep.

Oranges

Oranges, the way my mother ate them,
Standing at the sink, eating the slices
one by one in rapid succession, in-between
chores, determined to get in her ration
of vitamin C. I didn't offer to help

with the chores, only sighed and did them
grudgingly when asked. Enamored by the song,
Suzanne, where Leonard Cohen sang
about the bewitching girl by the harbor
who fed him tea and oranges, I wanted

my mother to sit at the table, her orange
slices on a china plate, offering me one as
we sipped Lapsang-souchong from delicate
tea cups. I think of this as I eat my slices
of oranges over the kitchen sink, their juicy
brightness on my tongue, an efficient joy.

Perspective

When a cousin had a stroke,
unusual in a person only in her thirties,
She was able to describe, after her long
recovery, how her mind struggled
to fill in the blanks, but the information
was misinformed and the answers crooked.
The tea kettle would shout,
and someone's knee would open
 its mouth and ask what was wrong,
and it did not seem strange until
she realized that this was her language
that no one else could respond to
or translate. Her job alone to determine
how to console the despair of the roaring
vacuum cleaner while trying
to answer the ringing elbow.

Tappan Zee

From the window of the Tarrytown library at night, you
can see the green lights of the bridge, bright over dark water.
When I was little, I thought they were strands of emeralds looped
across the water, as my father drove us home from visiting
relatives on the Jersey side. The new bridge will be renamed,
will shine with LED lights, states the local news alongside
comments including the old bridge sucks from some opinionated
Matthew. It's something, watching it rise from the Hudson,

this new bridge. My parents grew up in New Jersey. Our
family moved from NJ to NY then NJ to NY, and returned
to NJ. I grew up and went NY CT NY, surprising myself
ending up a local girl back near the Westchester town where
I grew up. It's officially the Governor Malcolm Wilson Tappan
Zee Bridge. Zee means sea. Years ago, just after dawn,
I dozed off in the line at a toll booth and tapped some guy's
bumper. I still remember the look of fury on his face until

he saw I was just some kid, still in my wedding guest
fanciest and he settled for shaking a finger at me as I
mouthed sorry through the window. It's a cantilever
bridge: a beam anchored on one end only is a cantilever.
I can drive from the Tarrytown, New York side to
Ridgewood, New Jersey with closed eyes if I had to,
all 16,013 feet of bridge. I drove home after we settled
my mother in the hospital, raced back at three a.m. after
the phone call about her emergency surgery. It's the largest

bridge in New York State. Feels that when you drive over it begging God not to take her tonight. When you drive over it practicing your eulogy for your father who surprises everyone by going first. They are buried in a graveyard beyond the coiling highways in New Jersey. I see them in mind every day in the kitchen overlooking the long yard where he putters. She is calling across the bridge, over the long stretch of shimmering water for someone to put on the kettle for tea.

Advice

The sun falls across the room
like a great calm love. I tell
you what I have learned from
the cupboard of secrets. The litany
of dark bitters like spent, sour rags,
the jewel colored jars of sweetness,
of beauty, of love.

That you can hold happiness and
sorrow at the same time. That
things can change you forever
like a hand raised in anger or
a great kindness. That you don't
have to be afraid that anything can
be taken from you, because anything
can be given to you as well.

Picture Book

This last gift, curled up and puzzle-fitted
into me, this sturdy bloom of a five year old
boy. Head resting on my shoulder as we read,
his hair is sweet, that good smell of soap,
and a day well spent.

We could be the bears in the book, crunching
leaves as we walk through the forest.
We could be anything we want safe in
this comfort. Turning the page, I prefer
our story, this blue and yellow room,

a boy in pajamas snuggled in, rapt
in attention to the words read aloud. As
the bears wander the woods, his small,
bare feet twitch beneath the blankets.
I would gladly fall asleep into a long

hibernation like the fictional bears, stay
beneath the glow of the stars pasted to
his ceiling, the dinosaurs romping across
the cheerful red and blue quilt. This
is the story I hope to hold in me like

an ember, this warmth, this quiet, this
feeling of being held safe in the cupped
hand of night, when I am one of those
women who pause to admire babies.

Mouse

A pet store mouse meant for a snake's dinner.
Bought for a dollar, stowaway in the pocket
of my child. Tiny muscles like tuned wires
beneath the white pelt, the twitch of storybook
whiskers. Thinking lice, sharp teeth, disease,
I watch it run down the arm of my child to the
safe cup of her hands.

Such tears for such a small thing lost. Delaying
dinner, we listen to her story. How she put the mouse
in her hamster's cage, how she thought they would
be friends. How the mouse died in her hand,
how she could not save it. Her father shrugs,
she will forget about it tomorrow. I know

 he is thinking of the long list of pets come
and gone, hermit crabs, salamanders, goldfish,
of the childish funerals in the flower beds we have
attended. She hiccups with weeping, stricken
with guilt and grief. I think how the little things
become a long strand in the mind's fabric.
I listen as she tells her story again.

A Night in the Country

Stars like mica chips swirled into a dense, dark batter. I stand
in the open space near the car, gaping at the wild beauty, this
unfamiliar width of sky. Something rustles the underbrush near
the stacked wood the owners said to use if the night cooled.

Inside, chilly, looking at the empty yawn of the fireplace, I feel
the blackened sky pour like thick tar over the cabin roof; feel

the rush of blood looping beneath my skin, The only sound
in this small space scratched in among the Fir trees is my
breathing. My heart beats faster in this panic that embarrasses
me even though there's no one to witness. My presence is an

intrusion, a flash of heated red lighting up the roof, X marks
the spot on this black hump, this mountain. My movements

feel like they bother the cloistered air, wake up mice long asleep.
The click of the stove knob to call up fire, the splash of water
into the kettle, all sound too huge in this crush of silence of no
phones or people or noise I know. I sleep clutching a flashlight.

Birds scrape away the pitch of night with their wings, carry light
into the dark folds of the trees. Rested air greets me on the porch,
fresh edged. Green perking up from every dark wooded surface,
makes small paper noises in the crisp biting breeze. The clean

sky stretches a long blue, licks at the cloud creamy froth dotting
this storybook morning, complacent.

Backstory

I am from the whistle of a tea kettle always calling
from the stove, and a Scottish calendar tacked on
the kitchen wall. I am from turquoise shutters
on a tall white house where bees hummed over
carefully planted flowers no children could touch.

I am from long sidewalks and the rush of commuter
trains, parks that roamed the rind of the Long Island
Sound, and the flash of bicycle spokes in the sun.

I am from hymns and Hollywood musicals, turning
the pages of sheet music as my mother played piano.
I am from the voices of my father's TV shows winding
up the stairs, better than a night light. I am from
Jesus Loves You, and Wait Until Your Father Gets Home.

I am from Scots off a boat and Midwestern farmers
with French roots. From stout black tea and blood
pudding, Grandma's Alsace Lorraine vegetable soup,
and Mom's By Golly pork chops. Hot chocolate at two
in the morning when my mother couldn't sleep.

I am from people who believed in love no matter
how rough the road. From Don't Be Angry Like Your
Father, from a dog at the foot of a bed. From prayers.

I am from summer beaches, and church Sundays,
from lunches out, and long evening walks. I am from
After Your Chores, and pull up a chair at that round
kitchen table, a plate of shortbread cookies and just
perked coffee, a conversation starting.

Late Winter

Sun yanking a reluctant day
out of its dark winter bed. February,
and the sky wears that strange light,
bruised and unforgiving. Each gust
of wind carries a reminder of frost.
The bulb in the blue china pot
fooled into thinking it should bloom.
Why is it so easy to break promises
you make only to yourself?

In late winter, days turn like pages
in a book that needs a better translation.
Someone has forgotten the meaning
of the words: sun, warmth, green, grow.
Slow work, this determination to see
it through. The trees outside scrape
dark fingers against the pale roof
of winter, their silhouettes a stark
beauty, their resilience a guide.

Elegy for Twin Daughters

Two houses—such luxury! Never mind the failings
of the dull minded architect, rendering both spaces
rectangular, tight and airless, with limited possibilities.
Still, the view afforded where they must winter: aged trees
admire themselves in the fine glass of the pond, tender

downy feathers catch in spikes of well fed grass—a small
homage from geese strolling among the headstones.
Their other place, for whimsy call it a summer cottage,
high on a shelf holding two pairs of pristine socks,
condolence cards, fabric scraps from two small quilts.

Strange real estate this dark corner lot the size
of a shoebox. Still, there's light enough, that shaft
of burnt sun piercing through the sturdy wood,
each time I walk past the closet door.

How to Burn

Walk through fire, wick that you are,
that we all are, our clothes burning,
the acrid smell of hair singeing as the flames
rise. Walk through the fire without hope
of water or saving or any kind of grace.
There are the last steps, the ones where
everyone leaves you, the ones where you
are along, little wick, stripped down
facing the flames, because no matter
how much they want to, no one can walk
this walk for you. You are forgiven
your first flinching, your tears, your regret,
your absolute fear, you are forgiven everything,
and still you must walk so walk you do
until it all burns away - what you knew,
what your days were, what your life was,
until all that remains is what you started with,
a wick, with the ability to burn and give light
to darkness.

Autarkeia

The sea does not want or need you.
As you stand gazing out to the horizon's
blur of sky and water, as you cup your hand
to shield an eye from the flares of sun, or
bend to toss that bit of rock into the fingers
of incoming water, as you pocket a chestnut
cowry, a mussel shell bluer than its brothers.

The sea goes about its business whether you
are there or not. The gulls, the only ones to hope,
watch to see if you will be careless and leave a trail
of crumbs to snatch. Beneath the cast of your
shadow, the crab investigates the new discards
of larger creatures stirred up by the small mayhem
of each relentless wave. Already your footprints

are dissolving their gullies of shape on the sand, imprint
of toes disappearing, then arch and heel, back to a
denying smoothness. The waves keep their continual
approach and retreat, the wind its restless hunt, and you
turning over a rubbery clump of brown kelp in your
hands, have never felt more like yourself than by this
sea, this place that holds no claim on you, which
doesn't care if you come or go.

Couldn't Get Up in the Morning

All summer it rained on me.
One droplet at a time, indoors,
on the desk, at the table, on the couch,
even inside the car. A random drop,

maybe two, of rain. It did not seem
to be raining on anyone else, not that
I mentioned it. I looked and tried
to discern from other people's reactions,

from a different note in their conversation,
if they too were rained on. No one reacted,
no one shifted oddly or altered their tone,
or brought a hand to the spot on the arm or leg

or face to test the wetness of a rain drop, but
then again, I tried to suppress any reaction
when it happened to me, my voice steady
and unbroken as any other voices in the room.

THREE

THREE

Yellow

In this third life, trying
to find my dandelion purpose.
Some chlorophyll miracle,
something perennial, not annual
in the scheme of things. Common
wonders these miniature suns, let
these brave little scrubs be
the gifts I offer my strange angels,
to show I am willing to learn
how to change from shine to seed,
to close my eyes and lean into
the wind, go where it carries me.

Pentimento

Looking up from my book to the far
corner of the room. A breath
of motion, a shimmer. On these darkling
nights, five hundred years or longer,
ceilings give way to firs, a glimpse
of smoke-colored sky, blurred, as if
the tips of trees have painted dusk
with careless application. Earlier,
I thought, I have not participated enough
in this world.

It's been rooms, yards, a crumbling
parking lot, view out car windows,
doorways, and halls with flickering lights.
All I have touched and loved, flesh
and echo, shadows and light, imprinted
on me too much and not enough. Desire
pins to the stars in this temporary ceiling,
calls to me sharply, like the solitary
fox that roams our yard, that bark startling
in the quiet of the night. I recognize
that sound: a voice in this world,
seeking.

Peach

Dropping my son off at the high school, I stop
at the light. Stepping off the curb, she is wearing
tight red pants, a bold choice for a wide-hipped
figure. She crosses in front of my car and I realize
she is younger than I thought, barely a teenager.

Stooped from the heavy back pack, she walks
slowly. The pants are tomato red, maybe her
favorite color, or comforting like a favorite soup.
She brushes her hair off her face, it's a sweet face.
The kind of sweet face that looks slightly bruised

like a beautiful peach crowded in the market's bin.
She's that age where every pain and sorrow
is marked on tender skin. I wish she wasn't
walking alone. I wish she was with a friend, that
the back pack was lighter, that everything that age

was easier. That my first thought hadn't been
mean. The light changes and I drive on, thinking
about her, hoping no one will tease her about
those red pants, and if they do, she will not mind,
maybe even laugh it off. But that would be
a different face, a different girl.

Poem for my Black Jacket

The poet reads at the festival, but
my mind frets, returning to my black
jacket hanging on the coat rack
 in the hall. I remember when we
bought it years ago. You were in
a wheelchair by then, and I modeled
the jacket you insisted I needed
and I said I didn't. The poet's words
are clenched with meaning, and I think
how the jacket is the last thing
you bought me. When the doors open
and I find it among all the other black
coats, the relief to claim it is kin
to putting words on paper. Something
to hold on to, something I can't let go.

Magnolia

My Twitter feed seems to be a long list of people
saying they have lost their mother, their brother or sister,
their father, their grandfather or grandmother,
their dear friend. I find myself weeping at the end
of these messages, typing the only thing I can think of to say:
I'm so sorry. Over and over.

We are still allowed to take a walk here if we keep
six feet away from each other. The rain makes that easy.
Alone on the streets, under my colorful umbrella, I feel
protected in a way I haven't felt in weeks. A childish fancy,
but I'll own it. I take pictures of flowering trees around
 my empty neighborhood, clutches of cheerful daffodils,
jewel-toned tulips, scatters of tiny blue flowers in the grass.

Nearly home, I see a neighbor has hired someone
to take down a magnolia tree. I stand in front of the cut
branches, tied in twine and stacked, and seeing their new
green leaves and first buds, I say, I'm so sorry. Some
buds have made the effort to flower despite being
on their way to nothing. I thank them for this effort,
this last gift. Even in the worst of times, we must
struggle to bloom. It's all we have.

Shift

If you hold a sparrow
in the cup of your hand,
a found one, stunned
by the smash of glass
that was window not sky,
forever after
when you see a sparrow,
you'll remember
the feel of the feather soft body,
the tiny heart beating against
your fingers.

Talking

If you couldn't sleep, chances are you would find
my mother in the kitchen at 3 A.M. with a cup
of hot chocolate or maybe a cool glass of water
depending on the season.

If there was something on your mind and you just
couldn't express it, you could talk around it, walk
the long road of it, and she'd be by your side, a willing
companion on the journey.

You could retract a previous statement, change your mind,
alter your view, and it wasn't held against you, (although
if you were prone to interrupt too much, you'd likely
be told so repeatedly and with justification).

I remember it because it's true, how there was always
a conversation going, even when from opposite points
of view. When things got too heated, she would say
 "let's agree to disagree." There was always time

to pick up the conversation later, over coffee,
over tea, across lunch tables, in the kitchen
or in the car. There was always talking
and so I continue it now, pointing out a bird,
or a lovely flower, something funny, or something

pressing on my heart. Now no one scolds me
for interrupting when I rush to share my thoughts,
although I wish she did, as I look up at the sky,
knowing she's somewhere listening.

Out of the Blue

He was afraid of bridges. He wasn't and then suddenly, he was.
I couldn't understand it. My fears are life long, born young and
bred deep. I know them like I know my oldest friends. How
could a person just become afraid of a thing that didn't bother
him before? I would think this as we pulled to the side of the
road to switch seats so that I could do the stint over whatever
bridge needing crossing. He had always hated heights, maybe
this was just a variation on a theme. I didn't mind, what I hated

was his stoic insistence on trying to cross over anyway, when
his giving in to fear turned into anger at himself that hovered
over the rest of the road trip like a sulky cloud. He was fiercely
afraid and then, months later, the terror subsided into that dull ache
of a lifelong hindrance. He took measured breaths and drove
over bridges, fighting his own inclinations all the way. I thought
it a shame, missing out on bridges. The rising arches
like unfolding wings, the tangible symbolism of crossing over,

just the very here to thereness of them. On a Vermont vacation,
I left him and our son bank side while I explored an abandoned
train trestle, all broken, rotted boards and deliriously beautiful
rusted metal work. I went farther than I meant to go, looking
with my camera's eye rather than common sense. Suddenly
I was stuck, unsure of how to move, the gaps of board boasting
of the drop below. "Here," my husband's voice surprised me.
He stood on a metal railing just inches away. " Take my hand."
We worked our way back to certain ground where our son stood
shaking his head at two fools on a bridge going there to here.

Lessons

The summer yard is held in the gaze of the noon
day sun. You squint at fractals of light caught
in your lashes. She is teaching you how to hoop,
or trying to, both of you laughing at the spasms
your hips interpret as that liquid movement

your daughter's hips effortlessly achieve. Swirling
silver and metallic blue, her hoop wheels to a techno
beat from her iPod, glints to rival the sun. She smiles
at your doubtful expression as she explains you
must thrust your hips forward, not sideways,
for the hoop to spin around your obstinate body.

It's August and the day is wide open under the plush
green leaves, but you and the trees feel it already,
the turning hours, the days shortening, the anticipation
of the next turn. She is moving come fall, there are boxes
being packed in her room already. You try to imitate

what she has shown you, forward and back, the hoop
finding its center and spinning as it should for one brief
moment before it spills to the ground. There are only
so many goodbyes you can carry in the pockets
of your heart, you think, yet change is inevitable,
even necessary. There is nothing you can do but try

to find some moments of grace where you can.
She tells you to pay attention as she lifts the hoop up,
capturing the sky and trees in a perfect circle,
and at her count, you both start over again.

My Turn

It's the dog's job, this awareness
of the yard, wary of any invasion
of the perimeter. Eyes seeking

the reason behind each rustle
in the brush, ears alert to every whir
of insect, evening cry of bird.

He sleeps on the stone slab, eyes
resolutely shut, content to let me
work his shift for awhile.

Arithmetic

Outside the birds are counting God
numbers - the count of good things. Seeds,
water, the relief of first light, praise that the nest
held firm. The trees with their endless
housekeeping are sweeping the sky clean.

On the telephone your voice is tired,
telling me it feels that all the days are
the same, pocked with necessity, with
demands. You ask as if I would know
the answers: what should we do with

these last years, how do we make
them count? Because, you say, they must
count for something. I know I am learning
to count with the birds, let go what was
lost in storms that came before, find

enough in the hot shower, the coffee cup
to offer song. How every morning I draw
back the curtains, notice the light or the lack
of light, always surprised that the trees
are still standing. I never thought

I would live past thirty, yet here I am
twice that. For me, that is how I measure
the years, what I count each morning
as I ready for the world. For me,
that is enough.

What Remains

Bone, leaf, shell.
Kindred each coil and slurry of seaweed,
insect-bored piece of driftwood, scarf
of seaweed, mossy fronds undulating
beneath cold, clear water.
Bone, hair, flesh.
A stripped branch has floated a long way
from somewhere, the leaves have become
veined and soft like an old woman's skin.
A torn crab leg dots a long script of shells.
Bone, flesh, shell.
Easier to accept change in this salt-blessed
place. Here where what remains
is a slow leaving, where
all endings become new.

Prairie

Open fields and wide bare rooms,
a broom in the corner, a wooden chair.
Light passing though the wavering glass
of the window you carried with you
all the way to this place of nowhere.

Handprint of sun on the white clay
walls. Here at the chipped stained sink, here
pegging wash, the sloping land, the roaming
sky. Plucked by the wind, a faded blue
shirt escapes the wash line, swirls up

 in the cloud-threaded sky, no tree branches
 to reach out and catch it as it whistles over
the flat yellow grass. Your feet walk over
quiet stories of small tunnels and crevices,
the tuck of mice, of snakes, and bending

to claim the shirt, that scent rises, mixed stir
of mud and plant, calling from the river bank
on a slant of air that will turn wild to compete
with the roiling thunder, coming faster
than you can guess or plan for, lightning

flash on the plaster walls even after
you shutter the window. You will
light a candle, you will wrap the blue
shirt around you, you will close
your eyes against the jagged light.

FOUR

Recipe

Stir half moons of onions
until a fine gold crimps the edges,
let it join the simmering broth.
Add celery and parsnip, small waxy
squares of potatoes, knobby earth-scented
mushrooms, long fingers of carrots.
A dash of pepper and coarse salt, small
green blessings of basil and thyme.

Lay five bowls on the sturdy table,
cradle warm bread in the basket.
Breathe in the fragrant steam of
the soup as it fills the kitchen,
fogs the window, where beyond,
things in the wild wood roar.

Fairy Tale

Something about a wood,
the entrance where trees front the border
in thick verticals of sturdy bark and outstretched limbs,
something about a wood could persuade a person,
a certain type of person, that wandering in further
would be to their benefit. That sort of person would
see beyond the first guardian trees to the deeper

heart, might note how the light tenders, becomes
rare, intermittent, and yet still feel compelled
to explore. Stepping past the first certain trace of path
they'd pause and feel the press of trees crowd with every step,
sense how a few feet into the woods earns a hush, lilts
an odor of decay, of things returning to their origins.
Above, the sky arrested by the fret of tangled vine

and twigged roofing. They'd breathe in the ancient air,
the breakdown of everything: leaf, egg, dung, fallen bird,
scent holding memories, but whose? When the wood closes
behind them with every tree looking similar and the path
unfamiliar, that person might turn to go home as the wood
circles around them, tree after tree after tree, and nothing
is known anymore, especially the way out.

Bears

Younger, I dreamt of bears laying wait in the tall shadows
of impartial trees, the cat glow of their yellow eyes tracking
my movements, patient, knowing what I did not, about the thick
woods, about the way the night fell quickly in a singular hush.
Hours after waking, the smell of pitch resin and musk of bear

clung in damp patches to the corners of things, injecting my
regular days with startled boosts of adrenalin, a disjointed shimmer
like sunlight flashing off shards of a broken mirror, light reeling
out in jagged splashes, patternless, crazed. I dreamt of bears until
I met one, and stood in the rank odor of his dissimilarity, a paw's

length distance, as he pulled his heft erect and snuffed the cold air
for the scent of my being. I saw the same shaggy pelt that I
remembered, clotted with old berry skins, bent pine needles,
fragments of dried dung. Saw the same sickening scythe of long
claws, but the small eyes, round and strange to me, dull as old
handled pennies, lacked the fine sheen of the marauder's
intelligence, and I realized I hadn't been dreaming of bears.

Offering

In the front yard, the pond folded
into itself, a mouth closing. Small
fish, gasping, strewn like a pocketful
of silver across the scrubbed lawn.

I held the edges of the yard in each
fist, shook it hard, lifting and letting
it fall like a sheet, my ribs cracking
under the sod weight of it. Water

spread, fingering among jutting
rocks, turning serpentine, seeking
travel. In the cool clasp of water,
reborn in the river, the pleasure

of breath gasps, the glass- domed
sky. Houses tilted and sank in, plates
floating as the tea cups sank. A turtle
in murk water, watching, waiting,

and I studied that kind of acceptance
among the ferns and cracked flowerpots.
The mosaic of dirt and roots entering
as the sky bled, I saw the waves

returning to the shore, saw how to
breathe in the slice of moment under
each wave. I thought how much I loved
the paper of your skin as the sun
burned through, set us on fire.

Aves

When I became birds
I became murmurs and small
movements in thick hedges.
A pause, a thought altered.
A percher on a lamp post,
a wader of calm ponds, a searcher
over rough waters for that flash
of silver to sate a hunger never
ending, when I became birds.

Watcher and winged, I moved
with the inclination of the wind.
I ceased kindness and excuse,
considered loft and current,
grip and balance. When I became
birds, I turned thief and spy, a mystery
as common as sifting air through
hollow-boned feathers. Finding
a new way to enter the world,
and a new way to leave it.

Shimmer

On her side of the boat, my daughter nets
extraordinary fish. Rare species, we think,
those gleaming iridescent scales, the delicate

feathering of fins. Trying to untangle them,
they reveal sharp teeth capable of long
poisons, and we drop them into the pail

with caution. I did not know these swam
in the same waters we did. Still, I urge
her to put them back, bid the fish to return

to their depths. I watch them spiral down
into darkness, the water deeper than I thought.
Tonight, they will swim back through the thick

black of my room, wait for me to open my eyes,
to admire their luminous glow.

The Bear Child

A gold ring in his ear. A way to mark
that he is possession, that he lives
somewhere that is not his home.

Taught to dance, the leather harness
tight, the whip snapping smartly at the dirt.
They notice his long claws. A jolly tune
and a clumsy shuffling dance that pleases
the crowd. Coins in a hat as a few of the boys
pretend to box him and the men laugh.

He cries like a human baby when
he is afraid. This does not
make them kinder.

History

I was English once, and proper,
my vein's inheritance.
I hear it in my voice, in the phrasing
I use when correcting my child.
The plumped pillows, the tidy urges, the dutiful attempts
to order the errant hours into a kind
of sense, all know I was English.

I was Celtic once, seeking the pulse
of stories, earth and water. I feel it in the stir
of blood when wind keens through the bones
of midnight trees, the sound telling of a far
light past heathered moors, strange tea brewing
in a kettle on my hearth while the elders
in the village plotted a solution.

Better to live English in these unruly days. Preferable
to take chaos to task, line it up, give calming,
reasonable answers. Pay no heed to the smell
of something starting to burn.

Mousewine

Swiped from the cupboard, this inebriation,
the house sleeps oblivious to my liquid eulogy.
Music weaves through my sisters' dreams, swirling
light as air, their turn to be held in the arms of the handsome
young prince. His voice, the rapturous pulse of the orchestra

as we danced, the admiring chatter, all sewn with the sharpest,
silver needle through a velvet night, fashioning a cloak I might
wear over a false gown. What was magic, what true?

I know who nestled in the cup of my hand just hours ago, that
was true. Handed over, a willing trade for one half night. Tiny
muscles like tuned wires beneath their white pelts split and made
enormous to pull so grand a coach, unable to fold back into
 the confines of a small twitch, a bit of fur, seed eyes.

My heart, my desire, dazzled by the spin of her wand, I gave
no thought of what might happen beyond the midnight
hour. The cracked rind, seeds spilled from its orange maw

on the black road, lizards curled up, bloodless, like dried, spent
pods, the rat turned inside out. And my sweet six, mouselings,
companions to me, raised on scraps of my scraps, sleeping
curled in my pockets, warm like spots of candle glow. Prey
to the greed of wishes. Left with a cold, useless glass shoe

and memories spliced with a heartache. I sit in my corner
by the cold fire raising a glass to the cleverness of envy,
the bites of desire, toasting small hurts and betrayals, mousedrunk.

To Complete the Spell

What do they use when the sorcery
store is closed? When the mare's milk
has gone off or the quivering eye of newt
has turned to an inky dust. The jar holding
hummingbird hearts is past its expiration date,
the vessel of virgins' tears is empty and yet

the vapors rise, the long smoky plumes urgently
whispering the names of necessary ingredients.
How to stir the pot when the cupboard is wanting?
Are there substitutions? The way we might sour
the milk with lemon for buttermilk? Deep in the woods
past midnight, might a stalk of wild millet serve

as a cat's tail? A sprinkling of milkweed stand
in for dogbane blossoms? A husk of old pine cone
for the mouse's skull? And when the charmed
creature limps misshapen or the lover
is inconsistent in his passion, who would confess
to what was omitted or altered?

Ghosts at Night

When we sleep and the house
is theirs once again, do they persist
with their old routine? The squeak
of the door hinge, the low moan,
the footsteps in the hall we blame
on the wind or the faulty heating.

Do they peer into our sleeping faces
and assured of our slowed breaths, lids
closed over the flicker of dreams; do they
imitate our actions, formerly their own?

Do they sort through the day's mail,
or scan the headlines of the newspaper,
sit with a remote in hand on the couch,
as the channels sift one into another.

Do they let it be our turn to be lost to things,
twitching and muttering our way through
an inarticulate dark, chasing or being chased,
the unexplained terrors, while they unfold
their shadow selves out at the dinner table,
raise a glass, pass the butter, lay a napkin
over their invisible laps.

Fractured

They never tell you the all of it.
How she felt worn and ragged
like an old dishcloth, so much to tidy,
so many to attend to, all those short
aggressive men stout with demands.

They never say how she didn't know
how it was before, the mother's reflection
in the cold sheen of the mirror gone
with that first birth. Her father's indifference
to his new wife's cruelties. Even the hunter knew
more of her story than she did, cut open with
that second of hope before the mirror flash,
this time let the answer be different.

They never mention that she saw past
the awkward costume, the witch's warts
and claw-crooked hands cupping
the poisoned apple. How she averted her eyes
so they could just get on with it. Her lips
moistened with anticipation, eager
for the bite.

Green

Open a window, open a door,
I'll leave my house, my home, my land,
to dance with you in shoes of bark
in tree canopies, my verdant man.

A crown of ivy, a basil bouquet
with dirt clinging still to the threaded roots,
yes, I will be your vegetable love,
and you will be my heart's own truth.

FIVE

Off Hours

I miss the vertical sanctuaries
of phone booths. Not for the ability
to place a call, but to take a moment.
Part of the room yet separate
behind the folding glass doors.
I understand foyers and mudrooms,
that pause between comings and goings.
Empty churches. The brightly lit
windows of closed stores. Sitting
in the car long after I've come home,
just listening to the song.

Solace

And just like that you feel blessed.
That's how they come, these moments
of grace - after a sip of coffee on a tired
morning, reading a funny text from your
daughter. You notice the light in the room
and the way the dog with his aching hip
is sleeping a deep comfort on the couch.

The first warm day leaning towards
Spring and you open a window, hear
the birds at the feeder, and feel a wealth
of bliss. I remember a hard day driving
home on a busy road and a man in a peacock
blue shirt and torn jeans was passing on a rusted
bicycle singing for all he was worth. Worth
everything.

You will forget it, of course. You will forget
all these moments in the sweep of a difficult
day, but you will not lose them. They are
the first brave show of green leaves in a cold
gray garden, the cat paws tentative but
determined on a narrow ledge. To carry light
to darkness requires only the smallest flame.

Grace

The walls of the world are thin tonight,
 I feel the hide of it press near. I saw
my lost children in honeyed air, beyond my grasp.
I reached into the amber but my hands touched
nothing. What is meant by the knowing
of things outside this realm? I know
how to walk though these rooms.
How to live with uncertainty.
I have trained myself in contentment.

Tonight the church of my yard praises
the night's full moon, as trees slash
giant shadows across the snow, and halos
of cast light from street lamps echo
the silver round of the moon. We walk
the dog up a dark road, and a constant

prayer runs like a thread through my mind,
a quieting, a sought peace. My mother
said she was comforted by a radio homily,
the speaker's voice spinning into her dark
room late at night, saying how only God
sees the finished side of the tapestry,
that we are only familiar with the side
of knots and stray bits of yarn, the unholy mess.

When the light returns every morning
like an offering, I offer thanks.
I don't have to understand the ways of this
mysterious world. I just have to praise it.

Things that are lost

My heart.
Two souls.
My favorite huarache sandals.
A sketchbook in France.
Innocence, and the desire to sin.
One earring only.
The belief in consequences.
Two parents, innumerable relatives.
My passport.
The ability to sleep.
The sweetness of my children
when young.
Letters and photographs shredded.
Thinking there's enough time.

Things that are found

Pennies on the pavement.
A tortoiseshell cat.
God in the trees
and diamonds in the ashes.
Gratitude, hard won.
The wonder of adults who were
once my children.
Hope, again and again
like a flying bird.
A long road of love.
Quietude, and the gifts of solitude.
Learning how to finish.
Learning how to not finish.
My heart.

Road Trip

In Charlestown, Rhode Island, we pass a street
named Memory Lane. And why not? It's what
we're doing, riding a long ribbon of memory looped
through Connecticut and Rhode Island, down
roads that travel that fine line of what was
and the possibilities of tomorrow. We first drove
up as lovers, then as newlyweds. Tipsy, we asked

a waitress if we should have a baby first or buy
a house. Walking the biting cold of a Newport
autumn, that baby tucked under my coat, and
then the next baby, and the next. The children
are grown, and we are back as we once were,
the two of us in a car, wandering without a plan.
Last night in Noank, a young red fox was standing

at the curb as we rolled by as if waiting for a ride.
Today a stone owl statue outside of a library just
like the one we saw in North Carolina, another
trip, another memory. Touchstones, signs, but
what do I need of those? I have what I need,
you beside me still, the air tinged with salt,
and our story still being written.

The Lasting Days

I would lend you
this honeyed scent, this
vibrant hum, this purpose,
bee driven and ever motioned.
I would gauze you in slow
time, grow you one note only
beneath the hand of the sun.

We would float from bloom
to bloom, open-mouthed, a chorus,
learning the music of each flower,
patient for sweetness.
I'd teach you this language,
and how to read threaded maps
embroidered in the air.
Show you how to find home.

Black

When I forget everything,
let the shape and darkness
of November trees visit my
dreams. Ebony slashes against
a water-colored indigo dusk.
The rough handwriting of long
words inked from earth to sky
in the language I knew before
life and will know again after.

Midnight Streets

Put on the long dark coat
and walk the midnight streets.
Let the cold air wrap around you
on this night opening into something.

Walk past houses full of sleep and promises,
where children mumble in dreams, and a dog
snores at the foot of someone's bed, ear
twitching as you pass.

Walk without aim or fret or purpose
as the cast light of streetlamps drinks the ink
of your shadow. A strand of your hair snags
on a bit of wayward twig, and your coat begins
to unravel, one black thread at a time.

Walk towards the end of this last road,
behind you only a scatter of stars, the rind
of the moon, the whistle of the slight wind
following the sound of your empty boots.

About the Author

Susan Moorhead writes poetry and stories in New York. Her work has taken rides inside Norwalk, CT buses, hung in gallery ribbons, appeared in numerous journals, magazines, and anthologies, been taught in classes, preached in a sermon, won the Greenburgh, NY Poetry Prize, and been nominated four times for a Pushcart prize. Daytimes find her working as a public librarian where she is happy to be surrounded by books.

About the Author

www.ingramcontent.com/pod-product-compliance
Lightning Source LLC
Chambersburg PA
CBHW070334090426
42733CB00012B/2474